Where You Live

Pushcart prize winner JILL McDONOUGH's first book
of poems, *Habeas Corpus*, was published by Salt in
2008. The recipient of fellowships from the National
Endowment for the Arts, the Fine Arts Work Center, the
New York Public Library, the Library of Congress, and
Stanford's Stegner program, she has taught incarcerated
college students through Boston University's Prison
Education program since 1999. Her work appears in
Slate, *The Nation*, and *The Threepenny Review*, and *Best
American Poetry 2011*. She teaches at the University of
Massachusetts Boston and directs 24PearlStreet, the
online writing program at the Fine Arts Work Center.

D1549754

WITHDRAWN

Also by Jill McDonough

POETRY
Habeas Corpus

Where You Live

by

JILL McDONOUGH

SALT
LONDON

PUBLISHED BY SALT PUBLISHING

Acre House, 11–15 William Road, London NW1 3ER, United Kingdom

©Jill McDonough, 2012

The right of Jill McDonough to be identified as the
author of this work has been asserted by her in accordance
with Section 77 of the Copyright, Designs and Patents Act 1988.

Salt Publishing 2012

Printed and bound in the United States by Lightning Source Inc

Typeset in Swift 9.5 / 13

ISBN 978 1 84471 909 9 paperback

1 3 5 7 9 8 6 4 2

For Josey.

*And Jim and Judy and Susan and Molly. And Maggie
and Todd. And Lisa and Mary. And Eavan, Simone,
and Ken. And Kirsten, James, Liz, Keith, Andy, Sean,
Maria, Laura, Mike, Miller, Josh, John, and Alexandra.
And Wendy, Gail, Joyce, Robert, Christopher, Lloyd, and
Rosanna. And Susan and Rachel. And Kay.*

*These poems were written with support from the Boston
Athenaeum, the Dorothy and Lewis B. Cullman Center
for Writers and Scholars, the Fine Arts Work Center,
the NEA, a Stegner Fellowship, and a Witter Bynner
Fellowship.*

Thank you.

Contents

Acknowledgments

Agni: "Coffee for Everyone"

American Vale: "Shape of a House"

Bat City Review: "Worth Living"

The Bedford Introduction to Literature, Bedford/St. Martin, 2012: "Accident, Mass. Ave."

Bellevue Literary Review: "Bartholomeus Breenbergh: Venus Mourning the Death of Adonis"

Best American Poetry 2011: "Dear Gaybashers"

Boxcar Poetry Review: "Women's Prison Every Week"

Breakwater Review: "Fort Point Crutch at Low Tide"

Collective Brightness: LGBTIQ Poets on Faith, Religion and Spirituality, Sibling Rivalry Press, 2011: "My History of CPR" and "Golden Gate Hank"

Consequence Magazine: "Status" and "This Is Your Chance"

Cortland Review: "Cary Grant"

DMQ Review: "Dream Aubade," "Dear Gaybashers" and "Great Day at the Athenaeum"

Filter Literary Journal: "Married"

Guernica: "Angela, From Wisconsin"

Harvard Review: "Golden Gate Hank" and "Preface"

Jai Alai: "Parties"

Joining Music With Reason: 34 Poets, British and American, Oxford, 2004–2009, chosen by Christopher Ricks. Waywiser: 2010: "Runaway" and "Ontogeny Recapitulates Phylogeny"

Massachusetts Review: "Ghazal for Josey" and "What Hell's Really Like"

Memorious: "Husky Boys' Dickies," "An Hour with an Etruscan Sarcophagus," and "Blackwater"

Mississippi Review: "Pollard in Nantucket, 1870"

Notre Dame Review: "The House I Live In; or The Human Body"; "The American Museum of Natural History's Charles Darwin Exhibit"; "August" and "Constantine"

Numinous: "Toward a Lawn"

Ploughshares: "Pikadon"

Poetry: "Kanji"

Poetry: An Introduction, Bedford/St. Martin, 2012: "Accident, Mass. Ave."

2009 Pushcart Prize XXXIII: Best of the Best Small Presses: "Accident, Mass. Ave."

2012 Pushcart Prize XXXVII: Best of the Best Small Presses: "Preface"

readwritepoem.org: " On Being Asked 'What is Poetry'"

Sea Change: "What Washed Ashore"

Shankpainter: "Monica at DB's Golden Banana" and "Tender"

Slate: "Ardent," "Runaway" and "Breasts Like Martinis"

Status Hat: "We Hate That Tree" and "Heat Shield"

Stirring: "How Happiness Works"

The Recorder: "Of Women's Testicles" and "The Health Adventure"

The Threepenny Review: "Accident, Mass. Ave."; "Amos D. Squire, Chief Physician of Sing Sing 1914–1925"; "Ontogeny Recapitulates Phylogeny"; "This House We Live In" and "My History of CPR"

One

Annunciation

When I take twelve high school students
into Special Collections, the curator lets them
touch everything, asks if we'd like to see
a book of hours. He brings out two illuminated
manuscripts, one with initials cut out
by long-dead stupid bastards, the other
perfect, perfectly preserved. He tells them
smell the vellum, tells them it's painted with powdered
lapis, flakes of gold on kidskin, stretched and scraped.
Someone's touched the first initial until it's rubbed away,
edges darkened, hazy. He explains red letter days,
shows them strawberries and thistle, golden vines,
forget-me-nots, Florentine flourishes, a green parrot,
a much beloved annunciation. Mary, suspicious
in her lapis robes, her double chin doubting, perhaps
one eyebrow raised. The angel's in crisp white robes,
green and purple wings, bringing her a scroll
like a fortune in a fortune cookie. He holds it
and waits, her raised hand not a benediction,
more like *Just hold it right there.* A peacock
on the facing page, Mary's in a mullioned-windowed
stone room: green carpet, canopy bed behind her.
Any girl would love a room like that, her red and gold
book, holding her place for once this angel's gone.
The halo more gorgeous than his wings, a little nicked
where the prayerful have rubbed for luck or piety,
the flowered border worn away. Other pages—
Lazarus fresh from a subterranean spa, knights stabbing
all the wrong babies—are worn, too, but not as much.
We love an annunciation, Fra Angelico's tiny doves
on golden beams, this anonymous monk's patient angel,
his peacock wings. She was just sitting there with her prayer book,

and look what happened. Something amazing could happen to any one of us, at any time. You might be that important. You never know.

Breasts Like Martinis

The bartender at Caesar's tells jokes we've heard a hundred times.
A shoelace walks into a bar, for example. I whisper
Sarah Evers told me that joke in sixth grade and Josey says
My brother Steve, 1982. A whore, a midget, a Chinaman,
nothing we haven't heard. Then a customer asks
Why are breasts like martinis? and they both start laughing.
They know this one, everybody knows this one, except
us. They don't even bother with the punchline. The bartender just says
Yeah, but I always said there should be a third one, on the back,
for dancing, dancing with the woman-shaped air behind the bar, his hand
on the breast on her back. So we figure three is too many,
one's not enough. Okay; we can do better than that. *I like my breasts*
like I like my martinis, we say: *Small and bruised* or *big and dry. Perfect.*
Overflowing. Reeking of juniper, spilling all over the bar.
When I have a migraine and she reaches for me, I say
Josey, my breasts are like martinis. She nods, solemn:
People should keep their goddamn hands off yours. How
could we tell these jokes to the bartender? We can't. He'll never know.
I say it after scrubbing the kitchen cabinets, and she gets it:
dirty and wet. Walking in the wind, Josey says *My breasts*
are like martinis and I hail a cab, know she means shaking, ice cold.

Dear Gaybashers

The night we got bashed we told Rusty how
they drove up, yelled QUEER, threw a hot dog, sped off.

Rusty: *Now, is that gaybashing? Or*
are they just calling you queer? Good point.

Josey pitied the fools: who buys a perfectly good pack of wieners
and drives around San Francisco chucking them at gays?

And who speeds off? Missing the point, the pleasure of the bash?
Dear bashers, you should have seen the hot dog hit my neck,

the scarf Josey sewed from antique silk kimonos: *so* gay. You
missed laughing at us, us confused, your raw hot dog on the ground.

Josey and Rusty and Bob make fun of the gaybashers, and I
wash my scarf in the sink. I use Woolite. We worry

about insurance, interest rates. Not hot dogs thrown from F-150s,
homophobic freaks. After the bashing, we used the ATM

in the sex shop next to Annie's Social Club, smiled at the kind
owner, his handlebar mustache. Astrud Gilberto sang *tall and tan*

and young and lovely, the girl from Ipanema . . . and the dildos
gleamed from the walls, a hundred cheerful colors. In San Francisco

it rains hot dogs, pity-the-fool. Ass-sized penguins, cock after cock in
azure acrylic, butterscotch glass, anyone's flesh-tone, chrome.

On Being Asked "What is Poetry?"

I ask that a lot, ask a lot of students that. Whitman,
Dickinson, Dietz. There are hundreds of ways
to say you don't know, most of them
pretty good. Anne Bradstreet, Anne Carson, Anne
Sexton, Annie Finch. Right now I teach *Understanding
Literature*. They didn't *Understand*
that people still write *Literature*, that it's alive. Bishop,
Pinsky, Lowell. It took me three weeks to make them
stop saying they don't like poetry. No to Baudelaire.
Ditto John Clare, Gwendolyn Brooks. *What the hell
are you talking about?* Don't like poetry. Don't like food.
Vessels, buildings, days. Don't like lumber, time.
Poetry: whatever we say it is. We're
in charge. Homer, Akhmatova, Frost. *I don't know
art, but I know what I like.* Here's
what I like. Fresh chalk on my hands, marking stresses
on the board. *a PLUM. a PURple FINCH*: three
iambs. Hopkins, Herbert, Fred Marchant. Then reading
aloud from Alan Dugan who, I admit it, is dead. But not
much: the *purple prick* of that skunk cabbage is still
erect in its *frost-thawing fart gas.* Bashō, Bronte, Keats.
Berryman, Ashbery, Yeats. Poetry means you get to say
whatever *whatever* you want. Your professor might close the class
with Dugan's prick in her mouth. It's poetry, so it's
allowed. *Shall I Compare Thee to a Summer's Day?* Sure.
Also, *They Fuck You Up, Your Mum and Dad.* What is poetry?
What is poetry? I don't know.

Great Day at the Athenaeum

A meter maid was hiding in the ladies' room, sitting on the little chair where I usually put my stack of books. I smiled at her, and she said "I'm just being lazy." I said, "I'm just going to pee." She said, "I already did that," and I said, "Soon we'll be even." Then she listened to me pee.

When I emerged we had a short conversation about how her husband swears, in which she would speak in a normal tone of voice and then just mouth the swears, like, "It feels so——good to be home" and "Hon, you make this house so——nice." She said she tells him, "God, hon, you have to swear about it?" "Yeah," I added, and here I was pretending to be her talking to her husband: "You have to be so fucking expressive?"

The meter maid was not ready to meet someone who says "fucking" in the ladies' room at the Boston Athenaeum. But there I was. I made her day. She cracked up. She was having a great time in the ladies' room at the Boston Athenaeum.

I always wash my hands, even when there is not a uniformed member of the Boston police force hiding in the ladies' room.

When I went to get my coat and bag from Doug, the man who takes my coat and bag, I said, "There's a meter maid hiding in the ladies' room." "Yes," he said. "She comes in to use the bathroom and sometimes she lets us get away with double parking. Sort of a 'you scratch my back, I'll let you hide in my bathroom' kind of thing."

The meter maid came out and said, "How long has this place been a library?" Doug and I thought it was a historic question, and tried coming up with a year: 1789? 1850? The reference librarians would know, and probably there's a plaque around here someplace. But she was asking a different kind of question: "Because the sign outside doesn't say 'Library,' it says something else." "Right!" I said. I used an exclamation point because now I understood her question and it was exactly the kind of question I can answer. "The sign says 'Boston Athenaeum.' 'Athenaeum' is just a fancy word for library." "Also Turkish bath," said Doug, who is the best kind of coat-and-bag-taking-guy because he is also a smart-aleck, and that's useful in constructing the here's-my-coat-and-bag kind of banter that he must have to do fifty times a day. "Yes," I said, "the Turkish baths are in the basement. On the weekends, 'Athenaeum' means 'Bordello'." Doug said, "Speaking of which, are you coming in on Saturday?"

Then Doug was suddenly apologetic, horribly stricken that he had gone too far, in that he had just suggested I am a part-time prostitute. I, too, am a smart aleck, but I am also a member of the Boston Athenaeum, and probably he's not supposed to suggest that members fuck people for money. But I was too happy about this instance of Doug being a smart-aleck to be able to reassure him. Also, it turned out the meter maid didn't know the word "bordello" either, so then I was horribly stricken, worried that we'd been inadvertently making fun of the meter maid's lack of book-learning. I tried to smooth that over by saying, "'Bordello' is just an old fashioned word for 'whorehouse,' like 'brothel'." "That one I know," said the meter maid, and she pushed my shoulder playfully and walked away from the Athenaeum, laughing out loud.

What Washed Ashore

Hello, there's a ship in the front yard.
——*Mooncussers of Cape Cod* by HENRY C. KITTREDGE, Boston, 1937

The Italian captain's body: frozen, one
year dead. The name "Orissa." Teakwood bars,
mahogany racks. The Whydah's gold doubloons.
Great rolls of wrapping paper on iron spools.
A bushel basket of piano keys.
Wool greatcoats, blankets. Lead wheels. Cases of beer.
Scotch. Rye. Wooden crates of chocolate. Gravestones.
An organ. Coffee. Bales of rags, a box
of herring. Lath and lumber. Rubber boots.

Champagne. Seeds. Pear and plum trees, nicely tied
and labeled. Drowned cutthroats. Pool cues, still true.
Wide sheets of copper. An iron safe on its back,
greenbacks protruding from the crack in its closed
door. Compass, binnacle, bell. The stores: tea, five
pound hams, condensed milk. A signal flag, half
a dozen cabin doors. A case of black
shoe leather, taps. One hundred twenty-two
barrels of flour, thirty-six damnified.
Sandy jute. Fine stoneware, strong slitwork timber.
Swollen firkins of wet bread. Map, writings, two
punch bowls and glasses. Boxes of bullets and flints.
A compass and pump. A tub of pork, two casks
of pickled fish. Moses boat. Bags of salt.
Molasses, cases of tea. An oaken chest.

Inside the chest:

nine linen shirts. Five
caps, a suit
of thin clothes, two undershirts, two
old coats, eight pairs
stockings, nine pairs breeches, three

sheets, a tablecloth, a towel.

A handkerchief, five wigs.
A sail, a cotton blanket.

Quadrant. Sword. Cane. Knife.

A gimlet.
Hammer, handmill, razors, locks.
A saw.

Three china plates,
a doctor's kit, some empty vials.
An old book of sea law
and some paper.

Particular Crimes

The man who burnt a city block,
the one who left a homeless vet
for dead, the one who raped a grandmother
for hours: they all turn in
their tidy work on time.

The *Boston Globe* on a stabbing:
hacking and *thirty-seven times.*
Sometimes I can't sleep at night, pull
the shower curtain quick to catch
whoever's hiding there off guard.

When they meet Iago, they love him:
he was justified. Justified?
I shake my head, quote the play,
write line numbers on the board.
They all hold the book
in one hand, gesture with the other
like lawyers. They know lawyers.
All in matching suits.
They understand Iago,
and they want him to suffer. They laugh,
discuss what *torments*
will ope his lips.

The coordinator approved
my proposed texts by saying
I don't think we have anyone
who committed those particular crimes.

Othello, Medea, Beloved:
Not one of my best students
smothered his pale wife with a pillow,
stabbed his small sons for revenge, slit

his baby daughter's throat to keep her
out of bondage. Not one of us
will scatter the pieces
of our brother in our wake.

The House I Live In; or The Human Body

*For you formed my inward parts; you knitted me together in my mother's womb.
I praise you, for I am fearfully and wonderfully made.*

— PSALM 139:13-14

"*I am fearfully and wonderfully made,*" says
the skeleton, exclaims
the skeleton in ink, line
drawing, engraving of his
smooth shaded skull, awkward
pelvic arch, turned toward the arched
door. The *Ossa Innominata* of the pelvis is
unnameable, unlike
any other object
in the world. Our skeleton's arm
is raised, he's ready to knock. Hello! Who should fear
me? I am fearful, and wonderfully made. Forgotten
in the basement, in the shelves that slide
to press against each other. Health and Sciences,
from 1836: foxed
Health. Obsolete Science. Illustrated
with engravings of the body, all
its parts: *The Skull, Cupola
of the House. One
of the Vertebrae. The Kneeling
Skeleton. The Hand and the Foot; showing
the beautiful mechanism of both.*

Poem About the Body

After the winter indoors watching the same
planes, same buildings, repetitive puffs
of smoke, I was afraid to fly without her, afraid to fly,
trying to decide if I'd rather die or live with her dead.
We are young enough to joke about this, old enough
to have our own doctors, who tell us after 9/11,
they should just pass Xanax out
like candy, bowls in the waiting room.

The poem about the body
is a love poem, poem about wonders, misery,
being relieved you found someone to grow old with,
being terrified that she will die. Both, relief
and terror, symptoms of love. Her body:
stretch marks shiny as scars, indefinite spots
on the backs of her hands. Broken blood vessels branch
like fractal coral on her cheekbones. On her right thigh, a scar
shaped like the end of a handlebar, shiny
as a stretch mark.

The poem about the body, the beloved, is David Ferry's
from the Bannatyne manuscript, the one
I copied out by hand that first year, the one that goes
Of love and truth with long continuance and ends *God grant*
I go to the grave before she goes. Comforting
someone thought those things a thousand years ago,
and wrote them down.

You are fearfully and wonderfully made. All of us—you,
me, her, David Ferry, the doctors, the anonymous poet
a thousand years dead—wonderful, capable
of wonders, of wonderful fear.

Of Women's Testicles

In a 1684 anatomy book, *Humane Bodies*
Epitomized, by Thomas Gibson, I find a chapter called
Of Women's Testicles. Outside, Bryant Park
in bloom; fragrant hyacinth, daffodils, tall,
masculine tulips, low-lying purple pansies feminine,
frilled. Inside, alone with Thomas Gibson,
I read *Humane Bodies Epitomized*,
turn the brittle pages, learn *Women's Testicles*
differ much from Mens . . . he's nervous, carefully
proposing a new idea: maybe these
aren't testicles after all. Alone, against
the received wisdom of *the followers*
of Hippocrates and Galen, he stands over
some woman's corpse, fresh-dug, brought
to his back door in the dark. To develop
the newest doctrine of the most accurate and learned
Modern Anatomists, he cuts her open, lifts
her ovaries out with his bare hands. He writes
in Latin about female ejaculate, where it comes
from, where he thinks it goes, concludes
these Vesiculae are analogous to the little Eggs in the Ovarium
of Fowl, since if you boil them, their liquor will have
the same color, taste, and consistency
of the white of Birds Eggs.

In Which I Start to Get a Migraine
and Think of Hildegard Von Bingen

It's scintillating scotoma; we know that now. Not spirits at work, not Christ
or many angels. No eye of god, no swirling maw of creation itself; just

a flicker in the occipital cortex, a hitch in the get-along, back
of the brain. At first I thought I was going blind: Sunday

Times missing chunks like articles clipped out of father's paper, my face
peering comically through where I thought things

were. Text swimming, holes burnt out—no, still burning, still
glowing at the edges, hard at work. I tried to read, to see things

by looking to their lefts, tricking the brain before giving up, calling
the authorities. When it happens to Hildegard she just assumes

it's a vision, Christ Almighty. Christ, a visit from Christ
is practically worth the headache. Hildegard: who could she call?

She looks around at her same old nunnery, now carnival-lit, strobed, ripped
open: *These are True Visions Flowing From God*, says her declaration

in *Scivias*—sure they are: Why not? God flowing, flickering down like
    tickertape
in the sun, kaleidoscope burning into *Metro*, into *Styles*, through her ceiling,
    licking

flames painted above Hildegard's painted head, her eyes
rolled back, scintillating flames in the vision, reaching down or crawling up.

My History of CPR

In the 1700s, once we could print stuff, a guy
in the Society for the Recovery of Persons Apparently Drowned
posted broadsides like our cartoon Heimlich how-tos,
except they used *fs* for *ss*, suggested blowing
smoke up the patient's ass. For real: somebody
should blow with Force into the Lungs, by applying
the Mouth to the Mouth of the Patient, closing his Nostrils
with one hand, while somebody else *should throw the smoke*
of Tobacco up the Fundament into the Bowels,
by means of a Pipe. At least they used a pipe.
That broadside says if you want to make mouth to mouth
less indelicate, it may be done through a Handkerchief.
Now I go to the movies, see Clive Owen punch
a fresh corpse in the chest. Human, angry with death,
at the dead, our puny lives. Imagine the first
time that worked, the look on the cavewoman's face
when her cavehusband coughs a little, blinks, comes to.
Of course you'd hit the corpse, of course you'd try
to force air in, breathe for the beloved, the lost
one, reverse everything. In Second Kings
Elijah mouth to mouthed a little boy,
revived him—maybe the first medical record,
first EMT: he put his mouth on his mouth,
his eyes on his eyes, and the flesh of the child waxed warm.

This House We Live In

The eye is only one part of the wondrous body that God has given us,

says Uncle Bob, going to the wall chart
of the hammer, anvil, and stirrup
he keeps in his camera shop.

This house we live in is made up of many remarkable things.

Next he shows us our heart, explains
it pumps enough blood to fill
a gasoline truck. Bloody beating heart,
shiny red gasoline truck driving
off the screen, filled, I think for a second,
with human blood. The little boy whistles, says

I guess God went to a lot of trouble, just to make our body so perfect,

bringing it all back home. In this educational film from 1958
Uncle Bob explains how a camera works,
how it's not as good as the human eye
God gave us. It starts with one freckle-face
blonde boy saying, out of nowhere,

You know, I think being able to take pictures is terrific.

God bless us, bless the kids who turn
to each other, say *Say*, or *How 'bout that.*
When I was little, my parents taught me
how to pop my ears. Magic.
Amazing secret: I wondered
what other buttons I could push,
doors I could open on the house I live in,
tried eating raisins with my nose.

Amos D. Squire, Chief Physician
of Sing Sing 1914–1925

Dr. Squire witnessed one hundred thirty eight
executions before he quit. He'd watch
their breathing, signal on the exhale, watch
a man, hooded, strain against straps. Then guards
opened a shirt, swabbed sweat so Squire
could listen with his stethoscope.

Many times I have been so overwrought
I was alarmed by the thought
that what I heard was my own
pulse rather than that of the dying man.

One day in 1925 he stood
at the edge of the rubber mat,
just within reach of the chair.
He gave the signal and the man
was electrocuted as usual, except
I felt for the first time
a wild desire
to extend my hand and touch him.

Dream Aubade

Not the familiar hours
        in the snooze's seven minutes.

    School is cancelled

        due to
        snow. Not the phone:

                It rings,
      it's work:

don't come in

      Hanging up, burrowing in.

we don't need you

      Not the exam with no clothes
                on, the one in Russian
don't come in all week

      or Greek. Like them both,
      only
         you were there.
                In the half-light
      between alarms I saw

      your body:

              familiar,
    beloved. My bed a question.

And the fit answer
          you
                              made there, on the blue book
          of my sheets.

Husky Boys' Dickies

WTF texts Josey, and I text back OMG. We had to tell Maggie what LOL
meant—it's not Lots Of Love, though that almost always fits. Major
emailed LMAO when I assumed his inbox gets dealt with by an underling,
some undergrad, assumed it was Major's minor who invited me to read but
"can not pay much sum of monies." Sum of Monies? I emailed back,

Who wrote this? Your assistant's a Nigerian prince? WTF.
For a while we just played with these, joking, like I tried on
Wicked when I moved to Boston, called Lisa Liser, pizza pizzer, said
Fucken, wicked, pissah, dood. But before you know it, it's part
of how you talk, how I talk, fucken guy. Dude. When my ex

student saw me she said Sick a dozen times, amazed, delighted, meant
it's super I've moved back, and, whoda thunk it, come in to her cafe.
She checked out Josey, my instant street cred. Josey bought new pants
for work with a cell phone pocket; the cell phone pocket pants
are Husky Boys' Dickies, which I can't get enough of, laugh every time

I think of them, or try to name them out loud. Josey wears
Husky Boys' Dickies. My darling, my husky, my husky little boy.
Hey, Husky, we say, around the house, just waking up, just bumping
into each other en route from basement to garden to kitchen. Hey,
Husky, do you want coffee? Hey Husky, Hey Bunny, Hey Hon.

When I'm helping my students translate Sappho's Fragments 1 and 31,
I get them to make a list of many-colored things, so they don't feel stuck
with colorful throne. One girl can't think of anything but Skittles. Terrific, I
    tell her,
you're breaking product placement ground. Then I ask them to think of voices
they love, the voice of someone they love. It's hard to describe a voice, but

I ask them each to try, put his or her beloved in the place of Sappho's,
    make her
theirs, more real than just sweet-voiced and lovely-laughtered. *You have*
three minutes. Get something down, I tell them, *some adjective or comparison,*
even if you just write the same word over and over again. 5:47 p.m. on a
    Wednesday,
me saying *Do your best* and *You could just say husky husky husky husky husky.*

Ghazal: Sappho Calls on Aphrodite

For Barbary Cook

Aphrodite, wise enough to avoid death; daughter of Zeus, who takes
the shapes of eagles, forms of polar ice caps: don't break my heart.

Instead, come. Be near me now, like the other times you left
your echoing palace to listen to the words that spring from my heart,

in your chariot, fueled by your quick flock of starlings that expands
and contracts. Gentle explosions from the center, the wild heart

of all they know: each other. And you: blessed, young, you laugh—
not unkindly—and ask me what happened to the light heart

you heard last Wednesday. *Now, what? Who fell out of love with you
today? Really, tell me who, and I'll haunt her 'til her tight heart*

*expands to meet yours. Did she avoid you? She'll seek you out. Did she return
your gifts? She'll give you new ones. She'll soon see you with a primed heart,*

*ready to take you in her arms. I am come: Everything's going to be fine.
I am your army, I am your conscience: Sappho, I am your divine heart.*

[25]

Ardent

Our English word "ardent," meaning "passionate," comes from the Old French ardant and the Latin ardere, "to burn." The original meanings include "burning," "red-hot," and "parching."

Today what I want is simple.
Sliding Rock, North Carolina. Entering Pisgah
the air cools before the long slope of water,
skunk of moss and wood, clean cool of water
all around you in the air. Particulate,
minute, mist rising from the broad rush, water meeting
water. We'll breathe it, soothe
these parched lips, this burning.

The gleam of pale quadriceps, skin
of your cheekbones, bones
of your jaw. Your body smooth, hot
here, cool there. Local lore glory deserving close study.

I want to give you green and golden fields, alfalfa, wheat
in sunlight, August, three p.m. In Kyoto, kanji are burned
into mountainsides in August. You can read them from miles
away. Old flames, boxes of blue-tipped strike-anywheres. A state,
uncharted country, a compass, sketch of map. Oaks,
soft rope of tire swing, wide slow rivers, campfires, coals. Oak
Room full of flappers, Luckies smoldering in holders. Piles
of burning leaves. Also smoldering.

A brickyard a lumberyard a wood fired kiln.

My lips are burning. No,
my mind. In my mind my
lips burn. I am "burning." You are "red-hot." This urgency,
open in daylight, "parching."

We're human beings

That's why we're here, said Julio Lugo
to the *Globe*. Sox fans booed
poor Lugo, booed his at-bat after
he dropped the ball in the pivotal fifth.

That ball, I got to it, I just
couldn't come up with it.

Lugo wants you to know
he is fast: a slower player
wouldn't even get close
enough to get booed. Lugo
wants you to know he's only
human: *We're human beings.*
That's why we're here. If not,

I would have wings.
I'd be beside God right now.
I'd be an angel.

But I'm not an angel.
I'm a human being that lives right here.

Next day, all
is forgiven. Lugo's home run, Lugo's
sweet comment to the press.

I wanted to make a poster like the ones that say
It's my birthday! or *First Time at Fenway!* or, pathetic, *ESPN*.
Posterboard, permanent marker to say *Lugo: me, too.*
I'm a human being that lives right here, decided
it's too esoteric, too ephemeral a reference, but it's true:
Oh, Lugo, Julio Lugo, I'm here with you.

Monica at DB's Golden Banana

I pay the five dollar cover, say to the bouncer,
Have you seen her whom my soul loves?
O
that she would kiss me
with the kisses of her mouth! Her name
is oil poured out by an unseen
announcer, before curtains thick
and spangled as the curtains of Solomon:
Monica.

Her banners over me
say WEDNESDAY IS AMATEUR
NIGHT. It's Friday. No one can
touch her. No one has ever
touched anyone the way
she's touching herself.
Her fingertips are ripened
wheat; dollars fold, extend
from our fingertips to her
fingertips.

Her belly is taut and comely
with ornaments. Behold her spandex hot
pants, small, forgotten on the stage.
Her eyes are doves
unseen, her mons
shaved bald, her legs
long and straight, gone skyward.
Her tan and silky buttocks part,
display layers of pink labia,
tidy powdered asshole.

From stage to cage to cage,
until last call, turn,
my beloved, be
like a gazelle. Your thighs are tan
and slender above your thigh-high
boots. Behold,
you are beautiful, my love; behold,
you are beautiful! Not one among us
is bereaved. Your arms lissome,
your grip on the brass pole sure. Your
knees roughened, dark
from kneeling. Your two breasts
are two fawns that lift
their pink tongues, nudge
aside your tank top. Your hands:
birds that tug at your
spaghetti straps. Pull them down.
There is no flaw in you. Neon-
bright. Fair as the moon.

Pikadon

Living in Japan I'd often go to public baths.
Women with babies, old ladies, teenage girls,
everybody naked all together, even me.
They'd tell me how *okii* my *opai* were, *desu ne.*
The wide expanse of my *oshiri* was *hajimette, desu ne.*
They had so many showers and saunas, whirlpools,
jacuzzis and steam baths. They had *denki ofuro*:
electric current running through the water,
between two metal plates. Before I could read
the sign I waded in the *denki* corner. I thought
I was having some kind of attack. My legs went
to a sudden, furious sleep, until I got out
of there, looked hard at the kanji. This was back
before I could tell kanji from Korean. Memorizing
shape, trying not to forget. An *obaachan*, bent
and wrinkled, smiling, waded in
and crouched a long time. I asked her why:
Didn't it hurt? Didn't it feel weird?
My Japanese was weak and new. I could barely say
dozo yoroshiku onegai shimasu, much less
"Aren't you concerned about the long range effects,
some kind of low grade fever, radiation seeping in
to the crumbly plaster of your bones?"
I think she told me it felt good, for arthritis and for scars.
I know she told me it was therapy for people who survived
the atom bombs. Keloids soften in the slow shock of it.
Like going home, I guess. *Pikadon*, she said,
showing me with her hands. *Pikadon.*
A cute word. Like bombs in cartoons: flash boom.

Kanji

One fragile scroll of practice paper left:
these careful columns, brushed in thick black ink.
Its buckled length is stored now under glass
and school groups read the first grade work aloud.

Chu. Middle. Ten wobbly cartoon hammers.
Shin. Heart. Ten sets of claw marks down the page.
Kai. Sea. Eight floors of window frames and drapes.

The case beside the fire door spotlights skin
and fingernails a mother kept, small proofs
that give some shape to absence. This small watch,
like all the others, stopped at 8:15.

A scorched and melted bento box. Burnt chalk.
Bent spectacles. A girl in glasses skips
around the room. She's touching every case.
A game like hop-scotch, tag you play alone.

She stops where everyone is stopped, to see
displays of mannequins with open mouths
and red translucent skin draped from their arms.
Their eyes are closed. Their clothes are torn and charred.

Their painful bodies present in a way
that isn't real. The quiet absences
in other cases make more sense to me.
This brittle page where meaning disappeared.

Each word became a small and separate flame,
the light drawn to a simple thing like dark.
These columns, now, of scorched and absent shapes.

This page survived the flash of heat and light.
The words were dark and first absorbed, then gave.
The kanji must have glowed there on the desk,
fresh middles, hearts and seas in coils of smoke.

The American Museum of Natural History's
Charles Darwin Exhibit

We walk in to bones: perfect,
delicate ribs of slow
loris, spiral of Gaboon viper. Some bulldog's cruel
fanged underbite. Darwin
hated Latin, school; he collected eggs and shells;

   he spent hours watching birds and lying under the dining-room table.

Now he's carved in marble, bearded
as Santa Claus. Thick eyebrows raised and kind before
his specimens, their jars of yellowed liquid, red
leather notebooks, pill boxes of crystals and bones. Jake,
the eight year old beside me, covets
this, wants it all. In the film, crimson crabs sidle up
to maroon ones, and komodo dragons embrace
one another in a komodo dragon pile.

When Darwin saw *Angraecum sesquipedale*'s
foot-long nectary—graceful, attenuated beyond
belief, he wrote *Astounding. What insect
could suck it?* He predicted we'd find a moth
that could. The museum lays out the long
snout of *Xanthopan morganii predicta*—
whip-like—next to the orchid's whip-like spur:

   endless forms most beautiful and wonderful have been, and are being,
   evolved.

Touch the megatherium skull. See
the heavy-lidded green
iguana struggle up his borrowed boughs, his snakeskin-skin
sloughing from his forelegs. His masseteric
scales as big as quarters. Feel the glyptodont's armored shell.

The reticulated python spine curves to and fro
like a river; toward the east, *tiny hind legs*
sprout, useless. To the python.

Cary Grant

This is the height man
was supposed to attain. It's all
downhill from him. Those silhouettes
of monkeys, knuckles rising
off the ground, end
here: Cary Grant in the suit
he wears in *North*
by Northwest, a hat, a cigarette,
a suitcase, things
that civilize. The cleft
in his chin a keyhole, his eyes
now onyx, now still
water, moonlit. His hair so bright
we still know what *brilliantined*
means. We built studios
and cameras, spooled
film on heavy reels, preserved
him for the ages, the best
we'll ever be. When Audrey
Hepburn asks him, *Do you know*
what's wrong with you? she answers
for all of us, *Nothing.*

Runaway

1728 Advertisement for the Recovery of an Indian Servant

I'll miss her smoky cooking, beans
in molasses, coffee with cream. Warm
mornings, her clean kitchen. Soapy streams
of fresh-pumped water on her arms.
Her *Narrow Stript pink Cherredary*
Goun turn'd up with a little flour'd
red & white Callico. Contrary,
very pretty. And vain. Spent hours
at her sewing. Everything in a birch
bark basket. Clean. She had a pretty
body, worked hard in the kitchen, stitched
quick, tidy stitches. Used too little
nutmeg, too much mace. In *A stript*
Homespun Quilted Petticoat, plain
muslin Apron. She loved the ripe
pears from the pear tree, glazed with rain.
Her hair in tidy plaits: *plain Pinners*
& a red & white flower'd knot.

Come back, beloved. Oils, paper,
whatever you lack. An apricot
tree, blue ribbons. A necklace to match
your *green Stone Earrings.* A dozen pairs
of *White Cotton Stockings,* a latch
for your door, lace, linen aprons to wear
if you'd come back to Pinckney Street,
this narrow brick house with its new
porch. Over the cobbled pavers. Neat
in your *Leather heel'd Wooden Shoes.*

Pollard in Nantucket, 1870

Half a biscuit, half a pint of water.
Joy died first: debility, costiveness.

For forty years, I've considered other
courses, how we could have stayed together,
lived. We put a white rag on a fish hook;
we should have cut strips of bait from Joy's corpse.

An unlucky man, my head on fire with math:
twenty men three boats sixty days'
worth of hardtack dead reckoning
shooting the sun at noon
at the island three men left seventeen
men twenty-two days hardtack
half provisions: one and one half ounce of bread
Joy dead Chase lost the coast
two thousand miles away
eleven men two boats eight
days hardtack ten men two boats
one black body to feed us nine
men then eight men then Hendricks
lost four men with the last of the last
black body drawing lots
the boy with his head on the gunwale
three men in one boat eating
my cousin's body   Then just me
and Ramsdell. Eating Barzillai Ray.

Half a biscuit, half a pint of water.
The locked cuddy. Dry
mouth. My wife is kind,
keeps a second larder by our bed.
I wake up with salt in my mouth, dream
of marrow, hardtack soaked

[37]

in seaspray, salt burning
my raw throat, split lips.
The boy's head on the gunwale,
liking his fate as well as any other.

Now I am dying, finally, of myself.
I still have my compass, *Navigation*,
the quadrant in its heavy salted box.
The paper will mark a quiet death,
a Night Watchman leaving behind
a blind wife, a house. A nobody
in his own hometown.

If we had used poor Joy's body for Shark-
baite Shoot the shark—we had musket,
pistols, powder—haul his rough
and heavy body in with us.
Roast shark on flat stones set in ballast sand.
Shark steaks to strengthen us, shark blood
to slake our thirst, strips of shark to bait
the hook next time. All of us
alive, steaks pierced on our knives,
laughing, eating to fullness.
We'd find wind, trim the sails,
run straight down for shore.

The Health Adventure

It's a place, a science museum, minus
the other exhibits, where we went
for field trips from Asheville City, Buncombe
County schools. Matt Gentling's mom,
the docent, told us the best birth control pill
was an aspirin, held between your knees. Twelve,
thirteen, we were too literal-minded, but we got
that it was dirty, a grown-up joke. Mrs. Gentling
made me stand up in front of everybody, next
to Perry Stamatiades, to illustrate puberty,
our wonderful bodies, these remarkable,
natural changes. An adolescent girl in braces,
a foot taller than an adolescent boy
in braces: just terrific. To prove it she pulled
my shoulders back, told me to stand up straight.

I wanted to die, shoot myself in the head
where she'd have to clean it up.
I forgive her. Once it was over
she dimmed the lights, and we sat on carpeted
stairs, a sort of anatomy theatre. TAM
the Transparent Anatomical Mannequin
spoke from a rotating dais, didn't move, discussed
her organs with us frankly, matter-of-factly
illuminating each part as she spoke. Her breasts
were repulsive, filled with squiggles of fat
like miniature small intestines. She's still
in there, in The Health Adventure,
looking down demurely, head tilted like
the Birth of Venus, but with open arms.
A little knock-kneed, her left hip cocked.

Transplant

Then, finally, you get a liver. Your hands
caress your new scar like a stranger's. Life
prolonged, gift from strangers' corpses. Your hosts:
benevolent graverobbers, Shelley. A tender
offer from the dead, from someone, someone's
family. New liver now your liver. Your
body still your body, still alive to tell
us: *Miracle*. Miracle in a dry-cleaned shirt.

What You Can Transplant/What You Can Have Transplanted:
Lungs, liver, heart. Also valves of the heart.
Marrow. Pancreas. Cartilage. Intestine.
A whole hand from the French. Corneas.
Skin and bone. Kidneys.

To transplant a hand, you start
with the bone: bone fixation, tendon repair, then
arteries, then nerves and veins. The first time it worked,
the guy with a dead man's hand on the end of his arm
freaked out, complained it was big and pale
and flaky, asked his surgeons to cut it back off.

Now they build Total Knees with Mauch hydraulic systems
for fluid, natural gait, and the Segway guy
wants to help all the amputees coming back from Iraq:
These kids have attitudes that you just can't believe.
Carbon fiber prosthetic legs, carbon leaf springs instead of feet,
Oscar Pistorious — *the fastest man on no legs* — wins
with his J-shaped Cheetahs. A man who has them
writes on his blog that once, out running, he heard
a little girl ask *Daddy, is that man a robot?*

Good question. The old saw about the axe, also old:
handle replaced twice, the head three times.
We eat and drink. We invent, evolve, take
from the dead: the body pulls what it needs
from the immense and varied world.

Ontogeny Recapitulates Phylogeny

My young parents, telling
us stories about biology
class, MacMurray, class
of '64, the year
my mother wore the turquoise
leather mini-skirt we knew
from the dress-up box, tossed
in with blue velvet, blue tulle, tasseled
white leather majorette boots, baton,
poodle-embroidered circle
skirts straight out of *Happy*
Days. We wore them
with gramma's veiled and feathered
hats, mom's frosted wig, imagined
the glamour of prom, or college, getting
married, having babies, growing up.
At the reunion, Professor Whatsisname
remembered my dad was the best
in their class, looked at my mother's legs
before saying, warmly, *Oh, yes, you*
sat in front. Ontogeny recapitulates
phylogeny, my parents recited,
remembering when they were
young and wrote this stuff
in notebooks, had notebooks,
memorized what dead men
said. When we asked what
it meant, they struggled, laughing, easily
distracted: dinosaurs, walking fish,
tadpole-looking embyros
growing into baby girls. We thought
we'd study it in college, but by the time
we got to college, nobody wrote it down
in notebooks. Ontogeny recapitulates

phylogeny: outdated as saddle
shoes, veiled hats, monkeys'
uncles, *Inherit the Wind*.

Preface

Hand and foot, from head to toe, the body we know
like the back of our hands, we say, patting our palms
since we don't know back from front, don't know our ass
from our elbow. I help Liz find her vagina to use
a tampon her first time, Brooke tells me what to expect
during a blow job, Jeff says to let the funneled
force of Coors hold open my throat, a stranger
gives me Valium when I reach for her hand
on a plane. Now Depo, condoms, the Pill
make way for FSH and BBT, how the sperm
that makes boys goes faster, dies sooner,
like boys, says Joanna, holding her little girl.
Laura's fingers flick to show how the dye popped open
her fallopian tubes. Rita Mae says a 48 year old's sperm
could cause autism, Esther says *kids are nice but they
do ruin your life*. Billy's friend announces,
out of nowhere, *I am so happy with my decision
not to have children* and none of us believe her.
X shopped around for the perfect Jewish eggs, Y
injected her belly, evenings, with little syringes, the bruises
blooming black, now purple, now yellow and green.
During implantation the nurses played soft eighties hits—
*I bought a ticket to the world, I know I know I know
this much is true.* She says in the ultrasound her ovaries
looked *like bunches of grapes.* Z has a baby at forty-two—
in vino she and her husband joke, *in vitro*
a no-no in the Roman Catholic Church. Encyclicals entitled
Donum Vitae, Dignitas Personae say why: *the human person
is objectively deprived of its proper perfection: namely, that
of being the result and fruit of a conjugal act.* The church,
thank god, is soothing, confident, ready to clear all this up. Life
a gift, human persons dignified. And we, most of us,
are perfect, because fathers put their penises in moms.

An Hour with an Etruscan Sarcophagus

Not the carved seals or gold libation cups,
mummies, alabaster urns. Two minutes
alone with this Etruscan sarcophagus and I'm
in tears. Nobody saw; I totally got away with it.

Something about the stonecutter's wife, I think—
not the rich couple together in stone forever, not even
the man who carved the jowly face, the woman's hands
on her husband's chest, chest doughy even carved in stone.

But the wife who knows they don't get an Etruscan
sarcophogus, that even though her Etruscan husband
carves them, they can't have this softening
of death, this consolation prize. Last week, midnight

in a friend's kitchen, I burst into tears over what I don't get,
wished aloud I'd gone to Goldman Sachs after college, how
then Josey wouldn't have to work. Rachel put her arms
around me, said *Shh.* Said, *Ah, Jill, you've made all*

the right choices. You've done everything just right.
I'm always wishing for money, for new siding,
just one job, a week off for Josey, off her feet.
But today, fresh from the Etruscan sarcophagi, I'm bigger,

wish for all of us, for you, for the stonecutter's wife,
for your children's children, such a friend in such
a kitchen, such a crying jag, an hour with an Etruscan
sarcophagus to think it all over, write it down.

Two

Three a.m.

Our cabdriver tells us how Somalia is better
than here because in Islam we execute murderers.
So, fewer murders. *But isn't there civil war*
there now? Aren't there a lot of murders?
Yes, but in general it's better. Not
now, but most of the time. He tells us about how
smart the system is, how it's hard to bear
false witness. We nod. We're learning a lot.
I say—once we are close to the house—I say, *What*
about us? Two women, married to each other.
Don't be offended, he says, gravely. *But a man*
with a man, a woman with a woman: it would be
a public execution. We nod. A little silence along
the Southeast Corridor. Then I say, *Yeah,*
I love my country. This makes him laugh; we all laugh.
We aren't offended, says Josey. *We love you.* Sometimes
I feel like we're proselytizing, spreading the Word of Gay.
The cab is shaking with laughter, the poor man
relieved we're not mad he sort of wants us dead.
The two of us soothing him, wanting him comfortable,
wanting him to laugh. *We love our country,*
we tell him. And Josey tips him. She tips him well.

Parties

Life is not one big party that starts right after school.

— Kora Manheimer's mother

We couldn't have imagined it, but she couldn't
have been more wrong. Sometimes
after I take off the knee pads and the house
smells like Murphy's Oil, I drink a Mexican
cane-sugar Coke from a glass bottle
at a clean Formica table. That's a party. I make
a nice supper, we have weekend guests, grill, light
the tiki torches. Cheese plate. Box of chocolates.
Crudite, crackers, cornichons. Galvanized buckets
of champagne, iced hours before the guests
come. Keg of Murphy's or Labatt's
and everyone we know. I warned you: if anybody shows up
with coke, I'm snorting it. No one does. Or
they're hiding it from me. No dope in the house: it smells
like boring. But carry a cocktail, a cigarette, from room
to room, witty asides thrown over your shoulder. Break
out the cleavage, all the jewels you own.
My sister's telling again how I tripped on her leg
in the road, Paul wipes tears of laughter with his new silk tie,
Jenny gives a good slow kick and hollers *HA!* Bob's running
back and forth calling *Near!* then calling *Far!* I hear Susan's
shout of laughter from the porch. Miller's slow dancing,
mumbling *Brady, Brady, Brady.* Strangers make out
in the pile of coats; somebody sobs on the stairs.
A boot and rally breaks the hush of the snow-covered, moonlit yard.
You are on fire, making Torontos, Last Words,
making everybody drunk. Cue the ice scoop, shaker, East
German dance music, Lauren shotgunning a Schlitz.
O, remembered Mrs. Manheimer! Cue the sparklers, smoked
striper. Cue the strippers, laughing on the kitchen floor at dawn.

Worth Living

Even when those guys rode the hot pink cast
aluminum deer, and broke the antler, it was

a great party, your wedding. Even when the mason, named
Jason, asked if I'd mind if he kissed me. Rudy and Sue reminisced

about that girl who pulled a knife
on Paul, how Paul talked her down; I called

the flowergirls beautiful as the bride. I lied.
No one could ever come close to Jenny in ivory satin, Jenny

in crystals, pearls. So we drank all the sparkling
wines—brut, prosecco, cava, cremant—and didn't want

to hit the amaro, or Patron. But it was a new amaro, and we forgot. Also,
a lot of beer. We're all sorry about the chair. And we shouldn't have let

Paul lift half the pig in his Prada suit. The next morning
I was fine, until it hit me on the Thruway. *Life is worth*

living, says the sign on the Tappan Zee—for jumpers, not for me.
Even that hungover, I know it, wouldn't trade one burnt offering, broken

antler, disappointed mason. Now, across the country,
mystery bruises surface on a hundred now-home guests

to mark the day. Woodsmoke-scented silk, wrecked shoes in a hundred
colors; our palatial, partial memories still glimmer in your name.

Alleged

I had a favorite student in the prison. He was my age,
beautiful, sturdy and enormous from lifting weights.

He was doing great, working hard on his papers, had
terrific things to say. Then he was gone. When I asked

where he was, the other students said he'd been sent away
for an alleged. I didn't understand, and they tried to explain.

Sometimes we have to work together to figure out what's prison slang,
what's legalese, what everybody knows. *An alleged. You know.*

They say he did it. When I asked what he was alleged to have done,
they said, exasperated, *The alleged!* What was I, retarded?

I quit asking after we ran through this Who's on First routine
a couple times, went to the blackboard to diagram not *It was a great party*

or *This is a difficult class* but *It was an alleged beating.* I took a little time
to outline *Allegation, Allegiance, Allege.* They nodded, into it now, taking notes.

One said, in an experimental tone, *It was allegedly brutal.* And I pointed at him
with my chalk, said *Yes! Very good!* and wrote it down.

Fort Point Crutch

for Frances Whistler

Whenever I walk across Fort Point Channel,
heading to Drink, I look over, check the tide,
imagine mudlarking there, imagine what
I'd find. Not much. At low tide once I saw
a crutch nestled in mud, a jaunty angle,
thought about the guy who tossed it, how
he gave it up. He limps along, then stops
and curses, weeping, about to jump, his life
behind him. Low tide, he probably wouldn't drown,
but I bet he'd break his legs and freeze to death.
And then the Lord suffuses him with light,
breaks the past open, relieves his mind, his pain.
He lifts his crutch up to the heavens, a sort
of toast, and chucks it over, all better, healed.
I was going to Drink to meet Frances, and told her, learned
she's an encyclopedia of loss:
the wooden leg that turned up under the torn
down roller coaster at Blackpool, the meringue
with both plates of some poor bastard's dentures stuck
in it, found by the Buckingham Palace gardener,
kicked under a rosebush at the Queen's garden party.
Milagros in Mexico, the new prosthetic limbs,
we share Ramos Gin Fizzes, Fort Points, Bees'
Knees, tell each other everything we know.

Ghazal for Josey

Josey shoulders toward the bar. The height of her enormous in her spine,
    her hips,
in those shoulders previously mentioned, now thrown back. Sudden as a
    paramour, Josey.

Amy grinning, Sandy still, Jen a blur of stick and hair but it's so hard to
    pull
the eyes from Josey's shoulders, arms. Josey's serious neck, sweet little
    hard core Josey.

Her hands stronger, smaller than my hands. Her neck stronger, thicker
    than my neck, skin
paler, more inked up than my skin, her name over and over—I'm dizzy,
    adore Josey.

She's a pussycat, said Amy, pulled me sheepish to the smallish sneakered
    feet
of this my muscled idol. I tried to be helpful, speechless, loath to bore
    Josey.

Her brother has a job at NYU. She's proud to own a church bus. I wanted
to talk to the base of her spine, to make her blush, to whisper, wanted
    more Josey.

Margie wore a bustier, leather pants embroidered S-E-X. Chris wore a
    jacket made
of feather boa. Beautiful women, powdered, coifed, poured into clothes
    for Josey.

Speakers give me a headache. I hate having to shout. But tonight I'm
    talking
to no one, watching, listening, small voice sighing in my core: *Josey.*

Who knows if my approach sunk in. A list of what I have to offer
    crumpled, damp
in her hip pocket. Scrawled on a page of calendar for Josey.

Are you giving me your past or your future? She said, she asked me, looked up
in my eyes to ask. *My future* for you Josey. Right half of May, left side of
    June for Josey.

The blue church bus belongs to Josey. It may be even cooler than my
    pickup, my love, my
light, my soul. Makes me want to go out, cut fresh lilacs for Josey.

I want to bring her mango lassi, fill the mango nectar can
with lilacs, hang her bedsheets out to dry, toss caesar salad for Josey.

Now the woman I love, on her hands, sweet Jesus on her knees, installs
    flooring.
I like to work with my hands. I'd like to lift you to the bath, offer succor,
    Josey.

I want her over me, her left arm a pillar I can cling to, kiss and talk to
    while
her right arm takes me over, makes me call out *Yes* and *God.* Then *More,*
    Josey.

Leslie said that I'm too femme for Josey. Jay offered other women "just as
    good as Josey."
But it's not about the "just as good" with Josey. Then Tim raised my
    hopes for Josey:

She's on the single side of things, he offered. When I asked if I'm too femme
he said *Oh no she likes girls like you. She's a top, our Josey.*

[55]

Top. I didn't ask what Tim then thinks of me. Church bus, laughter, that
   lift of chin, her hair. . .
I, Jill McDonough, have something to declare: Je t'aime. Je t'adore, Josey.

Brown County Courthouse, Green Bay

You didn't hear the trumpets
in the courtroom, violins
rising up three floors. Didn't tie the gauzy
bows to the rotunda's polished brass. You too
would've wept, beloved, at the mothers' tears, the baby's
small comment on the vows.

We lined the jury box and judged it good. Judge
Dietz presiding, his black authority of robe
benevolent, just. The groom:
his pleated bib, his shining shoes.
The maid of honor, guiding a spill
of veil. Our bride's dear hands,
cool and lovely, sparkling now with stones.

Flying back through Minneapolis,
in Minnesota, en route to Logan, I know
the firm line of your chin, your steady gaze,
determined. I will hold your dearly beloved face,
press my fingers in the valleys of your hands
for richer, for poorer,
in sickness and in health, tell
about the cake, the little quiches.
The huge Wisconsin cheeses. All
the laughing women wearing pearls. Orchids.
White roses, freesia. I will put my arms around your neck
and pull you to me, obscure
this brief absence
with the scent of your hair so
long as we both shall live.

What Hell's Really Like

Infinite, eternal; these words
do not hold meaning but gesture
toward unending, ample, bounty.
We're usually glad to have
enough. I've had enough.
My hands smell like bleach. They fold
the careful thirds of your shirts,
pair your white socks, tuck
them into your half of the third drawer.

Last month's dream: I went to Hell, descended
with a guide in a green blazer, a charming
undergrad. In Hell, she showed me
each of the exhibits: it was like
Williamsburg, or Spooky World,
the Halloween Theme Park in Foxboro
Stadium, but with a bigger budget. Fog
machines disseminating sulfur, rotting
meats. Each area evidence of our infinite
imagination: pits of fire, lava simmering
in kiddie pools, gratuitous
pitchforks. Rolling hills, each
with a stone pushed up or rolling
down. A living diorama of that liver:
black daws gathered with gobbety beaks, live video
feed of pulsing cells, raw, regenerating. Hungry
ghosts: huge bellies, tiny mouths. All
there. The staff takes breaks,
stands around galvanized basins of
transubstantiating ice, small
green bottles of Coke. I congratulate them
on their long success, how all of us, everybody
on the outside, up top, is fooled.

They love me, laugh, show me
around backstage.

Laundry doesn't end. It's something
we can count on. I suspect divorce stats rose
in correlation with our disbelief in hell.
Who, now, imagines anything could last
so long as you both shall live, much less
eternity? The eternal
silence of the infinite spaces
terrifies, sure: Eternal. Infinite. Not
silence, space. Nobody minds a quiet
Sunday, an extra pantry shelf. The dryer
in our small apartment tumbles
gentle, low. No silence, and very little space.

In the dream, during Hell's employee
break, I said I couldn't wait
to bring you down, show you
what hell is really like.
They stopped, looked at my green blazer girl,
wandered tactfully off. *No, now you're with us.*
You can't see her anymore. Matter
of fact. Firm babysitter
to insistent two year old.
Her hand on my stunned arm.

That Other Aubade

5:53 in the morning. We started drinking
at two; now you're snoring.
Mid-May, the sun's already up
over the East Bay. Josey, I love you
more than anyone has ever loved anyone.
And I wish I could give you a lot of money.

I turned the lights off to birdsong, stepped
sock-footed into sheets you washed and dried,
curled toward you, whispered
I think we're doing OK. We've carved
a small place, perfect for the two of us, in the world.
You earned enough tips last night to pay
seven of the nine thirty-five-dollar overdraft charges, plus
enough for a cab ride home. That bottle of red was a gift
from the bar. Astringent, sure, but good enough
for cheap Italian: we can give it two thumbs up.
You are adorable, still snoring. It's six
in the morning and we're grown women, figuring
it out. No one, drunk at dawn, has ever loved
anyone the way that I love you
in wool socks. Dawn the middle of the night
for you and me, this other kind of grown-up,
grown-ups we are, people we had no way
of knowing we'd grow up to be.

Toward a Lawn

Interminable
patch of dirty straw. Then,
when we forget to notice, when
scrutinies lapse, green's sprung. Oak, maple

have
nothing on this, the principal beauty
of loam. Slender. Brave
and countless. They thicken, become sturdy

multitudes. Rolling cool beneath a deck,
a hammock,
fence
to chain link fence.

So we learn the earth unfolds for us, can
shimmer with health under our care. Afternoons left
alone with your shoulders, tan
neck in sunlight, a shovel's heft.

Shovel. Rake. Roller. Plumes
of water: your thumb on a hose. Bats
rise, fall nightly in soft formations, consume
what could ever irk us. New worlds, habitats

form beneath the kiddie pool
forgotten in the shade. It cools, it will cool
you in its red and yellow shallows,
inflated fat and shiny as my breath allows.

How Happiness Works

Everybody writes poems about the Fung Wah. All my students. Mine's about the line outside the ticket kiosk in Chinatown, and how the little Chinese lady who yells SIX O'CLOCK! and runs around the corner with a crowd of stragglers, would-be riders, had already run.

I walked around trying to remember where was Travel Pack, where the Lucky Star. I found a shop that sold Lucky Star tickets, also lottery tickets and bubble tea. This little Chinese lady started pointing toward various crowds on the sidewalk that might be the line for my bus.

I shook my head. She grumbled and took off her apron and came out from behind the counter, came outside with me. I thanked her, and she said *No English*. So I smiled and gave her a big thumbs up, which made her laugh and say *thank you. Thank you*, I said. Then she tried to leave me in the Fung Wah line, but I got some Fung Wah riders to show her their tickets. Not Lucky Star, Fung Wah. She winced and said *Fung Wah!* as if it were a curse. She cursed Fung Wah and headed off across the street toward another potential Lucky Star line. It was a busy street, and a car swerved to miss her, honked. So I took her hand.

She was wearing a coat that was too long for her, so I only felt half of her hand. My mother's age, the size I was when I was nine. I took her hand and she looked up at me and smiled again, and said *Thank you! Thank YOU!* I said, and we laughed and walked across the street holding hands.

Across the street we could see a line of people holding the pink tickets that meant we were in the right place, the line of Lucky Star riders, but we liked walking and holding hands, liked the winter twilight, the relative silence. I think I loved her.

She took me to the head of the line. No one complained: perhaps the other riders thought if we were holding hands, then I must be retarded.

At last she turned me toward her, and we held each other's hands, both hands, and said goodbye: *Thank you! Thank you! Thank you!* On the bus, I sit in the best seat, up front, read *Little Dorrit* and fall asleep while the driver whistles, sometimes singing in Chinese.

Women's Prison Every Week

Lockers, metal detectors, steel doors, C.O.
to C.O., different forms, desks—*mouth open, turn*—so
slow I use the time to practice patience,
grace, tenderness for glassed-in guards. The rules
recited as if they were the same rules every week:
I can wear earrings. I cannot wear earrings. I can wear
my hair up. I cannot wear my hair up. I dressed
by rote: cords in blue or brown, grey turtleneck, black
clogs. The prisoners, all in grey sweatshirts, blue jeans,
joked I looked like them, fit in. I didn't think about it,
until I dreamed of being shuffled in and locked
in there, hustled through the heavy doors.
In the dream the guards just shook their heads, smirked
when I spelled out my name, shook the freezing bars.
Instead of nightly escorts out, I'd stay in there
forever. Who would know? So I went to Goodwill,
spent ten bucks on pink angora, walked back down those halls
a movie star. When I stood at the front of the class
there rose a sharp collective sigh. The one
who said she never heard of pandering
until the arraignment said *OK, I'm going
to tell her.* Then she told me: freedom is wasted
on women like me. They hate the dark cotton, jeans
they have to wear, each one a shadow of the other their
whole sentence. *You could wear red!* she accused.
Their favorite dresses, silk slips, wool socks all long gone,
bagged up for sisters, moms—maybe Goodwill,
maybe I flicked past them looking for this cotton candy pink
angora cardigan, pearl buttons. They can't stop staring, so
I take it off and pass it around, let each woman hold it
in her arms, appraise the wool between her fingers,
a familiar gesture, second nature, from another world.

Golden Gate Hank

I wake up with a toothache, think *I should write
about a toothache*, make it somehow worthwhile.
It's got everything: intimacy, decay, how the body's
busy, night and day, doing you in. One of the hundreds
of jumpers' corpses pulled from the bay had a note
in its pocket saying *No reason at all except
I have a toothache.* Josey's grandfather
shot himself after his fifth sinus operation failed.
Josey says Empty Nose Syndrome and I get confused—
how can hollows be hollowed? But then I go to
emptynosesyndrome.org, cup my poor nose
in horror, grateful for all I take for granted, can't see.

Golden Gate Hank hates his nickname.
If you wanted to be called Serenity Hank,
Ken tells him, *you shouldn't have jumped
off the fucking bridge.* The ones that live
all say they changed their minds in the four seconds
before they hit, tried to land feet first and managed it.
Ken says don't tell people *I think every day
of how I wouldn't kill myself*, they get the wrong idea.
I think every day of how I'd save myself, save
Josey: stab the bad guy, fall feet first, punch the Great White
in his eyeball, play dead in the bullet-ridden mass grave.

From the back seat of the Suburban, I heard
my mother say to my father *Driving across a high bridge
always makes me want to jump.* You might live:
A seventeen year old boy hit feet first, swam to shore
and walked for help, saying his back was killing him.
Another guy realized he was alive and underwater, felt something
brushing his broken legs. *Great, now I get eaten by a shark,*
he thought. It happens. But this was a seal, circling,

apparently the only thing that was keeping me alive,
and you can not tell me that wasn't God, because that's
what I believe, and that's what I'll believe until the day I die.

Heat Shield

We pulled up to a light on Tremont, just down
from Anchovies, and both looked to the right, willed
by the jangle, impossible racket shrill
from the car next door. I laughed at the poor bastard,
having been that guy before, and you nodded: "The heat
shield on his catalytic converter is loose."

I never saw, just imagine, you on the sled
in and out under a hundred Hondas when
you worked in the auto shop. You sliding out
on your back, those arms at your sides, your grease-stained cap.
Wiping your tattooed hands on your hips in a gesture
I love, even having washed your fingers' streaks
from twelve years' worth of pants. Shaking your head,
breaking bad news—*you got problems, lady*—
compressors, ratcheting wrenches, torque sticks, torch.
And when we first met I imagined, wanted, just
this kind of thing: some shared everyday errand
with crêpey arms and silver hair and still
the cracking up, impossibly complex codes
of reference, flirting, teasing. Quoting ten
year old conversations—*I love to travel*—
our catechism. Lines from *The Hunger, The
Thin Man, Candleshoe*: call and response. One time
a package arrived, marked *¡FRIGALE!*, enriched
our lives for good. How could anyone give
up on a marriage like this one? And start from scratch?
They couldn't. And lose all these good jokes?

Josey. Today you're forty-five years old.
Here is what it is like to be in love
with you: each day fresh with the gift of it. Fierce
nose-sting of tears, quick breath out of nowhere. Here's
the best part: each time, each moment you do that—

[67]

each heat shield, each first down, each perfect pour—
compresses, ratchets, torques, illuminates
the others, remembered or imagined. Each text,
each time I hoped for a future together, one half
as good as this one, its taxes and peonies, its *take
your pill.* Starting with the first time I saw
you, May Second, 1999,
in the Charles Street Playhouse. When I didn't know
seeing a stranger's face could do that. When
I didn't know you, didn't know yet you and me.

Three

Accident, Mass. Ave.

I stopped at a red light on Mass. Ave.
in Boston, a couple blocks away
from the bridge, and a woman in a beat-up
old Buick backed into me. Like, cranked her wheel,
rammed right into my side. I drove a Chevy
pickup truck. It being Boston, I got out
of the car yelling, swearing at this woman,
a little woman, whose first language was not English.
But she lived and drove in Boston, too, so she knew,
we both knew, that the thing to do
is get out of the car, slam the door
as hard as you fucking can and yell things like *What the fuck*
were you thinking? You fucking blind? What the fuck
is going on? Jesus Christ! So we swore
at each other with perfect posture, unnaturally angled
chins. I threw my arms around, sudden
jerking motions with my whole arms, the backs
of my hands toward where she had hit my truck.

But she hadn't hit my truck. She hit
the tire; no damage done. Her car
was fine, too. We saw this while
we were yelling, and then we were stuck.
The next line in our little drama should have been
Look at this fucking dent! I'm not paying for this
shit. I'm calling the cops, lady. Maybe we'd throw in a
You're in big trouble, sister, or *I just hope for your sake*
there's nothing wrong with my fucking suspension, that
sort of thing. But there was no fucking dent. There
was nothing else for us to do. So I
stopped yelling, and she looked at the tire she'd
backed into, her little eyebrows pursed
and worried. She was clearly in the wrong, I was enormous,
and I'd been acting as if I'd like to hit her. So I said

Well, there's nothing wrong with my car, nothing wrong
with your car . . . are you OK? She nodded, and started
to cry, so I put my arms around her and I held her, middle
of the street, Mass. Ave., Boston, a couple blocks from the bridge.
I hugged her, and I said *We were scared, weren't we?*
and she nodded and we laughed.

August

Parties out of doors, guitars, laughter
so close you're invited.
Buckets of ice, beer. Upturned milkcrates. Orange
tips of borrowed cigarettes blurred
against these skies. Nights
of Northern Lights, expanse of visible stars.
Not only supernovas: you've got
your red dwarves, your cooled giants, betas,
chis between the alphas. Each bright as yellow light
from your own kitchen. Each
one shining, present for the Perseids' brief tour.
Wake up again at four to meet
your falling star—falling star or shooting,
either way it doesn't make it. Either way
the poor thing never hits the ground.

Constantine

He mutters, laughs to himself in Russian.
He's crazy, Cyrillic backward Ns
and Ps rising up like ironed
curtains. No, not like that
at all. More like smoke, blue smoke,
cheap vodka kind of blue
smoke, letters blown like smoke rings
from the mouth of Constantine. Mumbling,
muttering Marxist, Trotsky. You hold
very still. The whispers expand,
assured. You remember Lenin,
Stalin and the czars, the tsars. Lips
close together, teeth clenched
as Petersburg, his mouth a wide
Siberia and just as closed.
Bulky continents of bundled
wool and fur ear flaps. He doesn't
have the beard he should but you
know it's inside him, rustling in Russian,
letters you can't understand.

Shape of a House

Shape of reflection. Clapboard, quiet sky. Or line

of twisting wire, razor shine. Color

of memory: value, hue and fade. Color rising

like heat off a road we almost all

remember. Wall. Duct. Rust. Shape of rain,

of ruin: rust stain, asbestos shingle, ripple

of embossed wood grain. Outline of saturation, decay.

Re-runs. Hot lunch on a tray. What the future used

to look like. Doors to some pasts avail you: *choose*. Past

those doors: rabbit ears, double knit. Dacron. Color

of nylon shag, Formica. Tricked out vans on Highway

Two. This slip of pale pours like driveway, that shape's

like a spill of your street. Curving. Also curved.

Valence of summer sunlight, bright and burnt

as snow. Stack of rooflines pitched as village, staggered

houses, arks. Emulsion echoes rust stains, rain.

Saturated as memory. Fading. Faded, fast. Surface

not surface. Shape not even shape. House not house, not

horizon: public sphere, containment, institution

sheer. Both blank and clutter: American. And vale.

Getting Shot on Your Birthday

It was a memoir class: read Saint Augustine and write about Youthful
   Transgressions, read David Sedaris, write Something Funny and Sad.

I was having trouble coming up with examples.

Once I called home and a stranger answered: my boyfriend had moved
   out and sublet our place.

They would have loved that story, The Shiftless Man and Getting Done
   Wrong being favorite themes, but when you teach in prisons you're
   warned not to talk too much about yourself.

So I didn't say anything, just waited it out, sat on a table and swung my
   legs, smiled while they shook their heads and frowned.

Finally, a woman I'll call Andrea said *You mean like the time I got shot on my
   birthday?*

And we all laughed and made the sympathetic sounds that mean *Poor
   Andrea!*

Andrea was delighted to have gotten something so right.

I was so drunk, she told us, *I didn't even know I'd been hit.*

Wrecked my new blouse she added, while we're laughing so hard we're in
   tears.

Coffee for Everyone

The cup exotic in your same old hands, so warm,
almost normal after the night you had. Holding
a paper cup to your mouth, your poor
bleared eyes, your forehead, is American, our gesture.
What have you done? An empty table, a paper cup
of coffee. A small room filled with the knowledge of good,
of freshly ground. Wake up: in America we have
plenty. There's coffee for everyone, even for you.
According to the Washington Post, *he was enticed*
with Starbucks coffee. Food when you asked for it,
all the coffee you could drink. We are American enough
to think, right off, of the ad we should make
for Starbucks: quick, cinematic cuts of a desert,
a middle-of-the-night rendition. Our brave soldiers in green
night vision—GO! GO! GO!—surprising you in your
spider hole. Then the flight: hooded you in a cavernous cargo
hold, circled by special ops, enormous guns. Cut back
to you dragged off the plane and past the barking dogs. Split
seconds of razor wire, bars, interrogation rooms. Gradual rise
of quiet, the calm of a *fait accompli*ed, then birdsong, the smell—not
smell, *aroma*—of good hot American coffee, $9.95
a pound. Your fat, hairy hands, cuffed to the table, wrapped
around the familiar paper cup, close up: benevolent
goddess, ring of night-vision green. Then a hush falls, hush
at the pivot of a nation, the center of a century's legal thought's
near undoing. And you weep, strain to hold the cup
to your sorry face, tell us everything we want to know.

This Is Your Chance

English Composition at South Middlesex Correctional Center.
Julie reads out loud, and I praise her super thesis, then show
how her paragraphs veer away from it, just summarize.
And is she pissed! Too pissed to listen when her classmates try
to help. Amanda offers Act 2 Scene 1—"Now I do love her
too"—as evidence of Iago's state of mind. But Julie's
shutting down, frowning at her handwritten draft, writing
that took her weeks. *Hey Julie,* I say. Julie doesn't look up.
Says *What.* Says *I hate this stupid paper now.* So I say
*Hey Julie. Amanda's helping you—write down
what she's saying.* She says *I'm aggravated.* I think
they take classes on naming their feelings. I say *I know it
but you need to pull it together, or you'll end up screwing
yourself. This is your chance.* We're all quiet, breathing
together, willing her to break out of this. Then:
a little miracle. I look around the room and see
that everyone is beautiful. Each did something special
with her hair. *Hey,* I say, again. I say *hey* a lot in prison.
Hey wait a minute. What's up with everybody's hair?
Mabel got a haircut. Ellie's hair is long and black and gleaming
down her back, Amanda's in French braids. Julie's freshly
blonde, down to the roots. *You guys all look great!*
They laugh. They're happy I noticed.
Thank god I noticed; now, for a minute, we
are women in a room, talking about their hair. Julie says
Amanda did her highlights, and Sandy blew it out. *Good job, guys;
she looks great.* And then I say, *Julie. Look at you
all pissed off over your paper when you're so lucky!
Look at all these good friends you have. Helping
with your paper, doing your hair . . .* She nods.
She looks me in the eye, back with us, back on track.
I know, she says. *I need to work on my gratitude.*

Toddler Christ

The year I lived in New York, I went with Susan
to see the Caravaggios at the Met, then
went back by myself, just for this one, in the corner.
Christ as a toddler, a little heavy, held
in a tired Mary's arms. Mary's got dark circles
under her eyes, looks at the toddler Jesus. Joseph and a little
John the Baptist look at him, too. I had a file in my head
for images of the baby Jesus, images of Christ on the cross,
the big-blue-eyed blonde in soft focus, gold frames.
But the toddler Christ, solemn, curious, maybe just up
from his nap, his plump limbs, tired teenaged mom
made me think, surprised, *we killed him*, our human
bodies human things, filled with rage and vengeance,
satisfaction when we've killed the broken toddlers long grown up.

Villon's Epitaph

Brother humans, who'll be here when we're gone,
Don't let your hearts turn so hard against us.
If you have pity for us, the poor ones,
God's more likely to grant you his mercies.
You see here, strung up, five or six of us:
You see our flesh, which we have fed so well.
It was slowly devoured, after it swelled.
And we, the bones, are now just dust and ash.
Don't laugh: we're already miserable.
Just pray that God cuts all of us some slack.

Don't be insulted if we call you some
Kin to us, brothers. We're sure that justice
Was done in our deaths, but not everyone
Has the sense to avoid being reckless.
So you stand up for us, since we're helpless:
Talk to the Son of the Virgin and He'll
Listen: He'll pour out grace in liberal
Doses, save us from Hell's thunderous crash.
We're dead now. Don't make fun or give us hell;
Just pray that God cuts all of us some slack.

We never rest. We're never left alone:
First we're here, then there, as the wind changes.
Swinging corpses is its idea of fun.
The rain has soaked us through and laundered us.
The sun has dried us out and blackened us.
Crows and ravens have plucked out our eyeballs
And pulled our beards and eyebrows out as well.
We're pocked as thimbles from the birds' attacks:
Don't do what we've done: see how far we fell?
Just pray that God cuts all of us some slack.

Prince Jesus, you are master over all:
Help us; make sure that we don't go to Hell.
We have no dealings there, and that's a fact.
Men, it's no good mocking: it's not His will.
Just pray that God cuts all of us some slack.

Status

It took me a while to notice. Then it was years
before I got it, knew what I was seeing.
One of the women, one of the ones with blue
eyeliner, explained it to me herself. The newer
prisoners can't wear makeup, a red-strapped bra,
but the rules have changed, and you keep the rules
you started with. You get grandfathered in.
A woman with mascara, say, the same
black liner, ice-blue frosty shadow she wore
when she was sentenced. A strip of turquoise lace
exposed, the collar of her prison-issued
sweats torn off to show it off—you see
that, you know she's been in at least ten years.
Probably murder. There must be such a code
to break in prisons for men, besides the tattooed
tears, scars, just being old, but I don't know
it. When you live in cities you judge the people
who don't know how to use a sidewalk. Tourists
walk four abreast, stop short, take up your space.
Look scared from a block away. Nobody in San
Francisco says "Frisco." Invisible customs,
clear to the locals; prison, a place where you live.

Assignment

Tuesday morning in the still yard. Mums
sculptural with frost. Pencil sketch of razor wire: gray
line, gray sky. Squeak and crunch of first snow.

A travel mug of coffee, tank of diesel: I grew up to be someone who drives
in traffic, teaches in prisons. Wonder of snow, of routine. So this
is adulthood: prison classrooms, chalk, wool pants, pentameter.

Twenty years since I felt trapped in a snow suit: torn
red nylon, the coarse matte grit of a cheap zipper weak and quick
to catch cold fingers, the sheltered neck, staticky hair in synthetic knit cap.

No silver locket with gold filigree, no ivory cameo framed
in twists of purple enamel, no skirt hand-stitched from an antique silk
kimono, its pebble pattern swirling and falling like snow. This

is my offering: taking the roll, instructing six women
to write tercets on snow, the past and the present, gifts
they've received, and other gifts they've given.

Habed

At the women's prison, I get M.'s late homework, ask
was she sick last week. *I got habed,* she says. She shrugs.

You got what? I say, a little alarmed, although
not much; she's not upset, so getting habed

can't be like getting raped. *Habed,* she says, speaking up
and slowing down. She thinks I haven't heard

her; she's not a native speaker, so she's used to repeating
herself. Getting habed's so normal it doesn't occur

to her that I might need some help. *I don't
know what that means,* I say, and all the ladies

hear it, get excited—they never know more
than me. D. doesn't buy it: *Come on,* she says,

you know. She got habed. She went to court. I say
a sharp *I'm sorry, what?* if they say *I ain't*

got mines, or *she don't know nothing,* so D. is on
her guard, unsure if I'm busting their chops or what.

My heart is still. I get it. I'm seeing language
in action: this isn't slang to them. *She went*

to court on a writ of habeas corpus, I say,
and they nod, and laugh some more, and take their seats.

Present

Months of apparitions: you,
flashing real in jeans, in sturdy boots.
Posture conjured at the bar
as I lean open heavy doors. Your
swagger, tilted head across Grand Central,
South Station, every platform, terminal, lot.
Fool's gold, foreshadowing actual you
manifest in doorways, come back home.

Practice. Preparation for your imminent re-entry.
When you see me, your face becomes younger.
Synapses snap to, fire up visible recognition.

Class today: no one's absent. Circle of ancient desks,
layered digs of graffiti: U2,
fuck this, Duran Duran, Andre
the Giant Has a Posse. The steam heat's
clanking hiss familiar. We know these
snug rooms, breathe wet wool, old books,
chalk. In that stillness—me talking, students
taking careful notes—I saw you. Sudden,
toppling vision. Not as you will be
on your return, but as you were:
your hands on my bare shoulders, your
weight tipping me over, down to the fresh
mown grass of August. The sharp crack of the
seven dollar resin chair's breaking,
resonant, permanent. You'll
come back. You'll know me anywhere.

Bartholomeus Breenbergh:
Venus Mourning the Death of Adonis

He's naked, pale. His clothes forgotten now.
His body's heft on sheets, held in her arms.
This small unseemly Venus, hair in pearls;
her face is red and ugly as a wound.
A scarf is lofting up, beyond the frame:
the black silk rises as her swans touch ground.
Adonis cannot speak or move or hear:
his blood is spilling, prodigal and red.
Her body's strange; her breasts are high, misplaced,
as if she slipped into this human form
in transit, her swans flying to his death.
A cherub sobs, small ducky wings behind
his toddler's back, his little fists to eyes.
Two hunting dogs look back the way they came,
their noses in the air to find that boar.
The golden chariot, its scallop shell
and silent wheels, waits in falling leaves
for Venus. Furious at death and grief.
Mortality: a waste of time. The swans
are bored. The night is rising up behind
the wing span of their patience. They can't see
what she sees, this pale man that Venus loves.

We Hate That Tree

This is the maple we hated
even in summer, even when its leaves
filtered light, dappled

our whole yard green. Even
when soft bats flitted through it
in August, eating mosquitoes we read

would give us West Nile. We hated
this maple with mattocks, hacking
through roots to dig any kind of hole.

The roots, we read,
stole water from our grass,
the *kalmia nipmuck* I ordered, the *cornus*

kousa, cercis canadensis I bought on sale.
Slender trees we loved, great shady maple
we've always hated. The neighbor's maple, planted

by his young mother fifty years ago, when Mrs. Ryan
lived in our house. Everybody hated Mrs. Ryan.
She hated the Lombardos, poured salt

water on an innocent sapling, but it flourished,
fed on spite and salt. Salt
water on a sapling: who would do such a thing?

We guess we probably would. We cheered
for the men who came in hardhats, insulated overalls,
men with ropes and chainsaws, handsaws, a chipper

on our street. We made them coffee, asked
what we could do. Men in hardhats, men
in watchcaps commemorating Superbowl XXXVI,

men laughing, getting sawdust on our roof and on the neighbors':
we love you, love your chipper, love your chainsaw,
love all your Pats and Red Sox, hate that maple. Hate that tree.

Where You Live

In the waiting rooms of our prisons, women wait
with well-dressed kids. The kids
are cuter here, somehow, than any body has a right
to be. I get in first, but no one's angry; I look
like a nice lady, smile at the babies, carry books
but no briefcase, don't wear a lawyer's suit. Going in
to talk about *Othello* with rapists, murderers,
con-men, thieves; all men defined by what they did
one time, now a long time ago. Prison: a place
where people live. It might be nice to know
your neighbors are reading Shakespeare instead
of carving a shiv. Where you live it's sunny, where I live,
today, it's not. When Josey was offered that stake in the bar
in L.A., we were instant Los Angelenos in our minds.
How quickly it happens, Eliot Spitzer behind bars
in an instant, Cheney arrested in Spain. All of us
imagining him there. Our imagined house with its imagined
Meyer lemon tree, the hard time we had parking
our imaginary car. How then can anyone imagine it's so hard
to change? The students in the prison: scholars as soon
as they sign up. Their children, poets as soon as they
rhyme. *I want to be a writer*, people tell me, and I nod.
Me too. Now, write. Prisons, hospitals, schools, the great
cities, their one-way streets and festivals; we put
our bodies there together, upright and seated,
walking along the hallways built to human scale,
sitting in rooms designed around imagined hordes of you.
Prison cell, cathedral: we imagined them, invented. Built them
around our bodies, or the bodies those spaces would hold.

Blackwater

For gifts beguile men's minds and their deeds as well.
　　　　　　　　— *The Returns*, Fragment 5, tr. HUGH G. EVELYN-WHITE

The *Nostoi*, the lost Greek epic of vets come home,
is only still around in what someone worked
to save. Some summary, a line or two.
For gifts beguile men's minds and their deeds as well:
one shred kept out of five lost volumes, words
distilled from our whole huge history of heroes, minds
and deeds, our whole idea of home. These days
we need some whole ideas. The ground around
us shifts for female veterans, fighter drones,
black ops, defense contractors, other pairs
of words we haven't reconciled yet.
So many now returning from so much.
Even Blackwater's founder—Erik Prince!
his name as hard to believe as his Hitler bangs—
says his employees aren't *mercenaries*, they're
loyal Americans. Forget the fact
that sometimes they're from Chile, Bosnia,
wherever. Look at "mercenary." From
the Latin *merces*: payment, reward, cost.
From *mercenarius*, or "hireling" in
King James' Gospel of John: The shepherd or
the hireling, who should we choose to watch over the sheep?
Back out of all this now too much for us
there was a river, cool and slow and stained
with spruce and hemlock. Blackwater River, Great
Dismal Swamp. And Prince bought the land, and took
the name. Perfect: you can't make this stuff up.
For gifts beguile men's minds and their deeds as well:
so many tried to warn us, give us this gift
clear as black water, as minds and deeds and home.

Angela, From Wisconsin

The cute waitress at the Alembic has
hair red as Ann Margaret's, eyes liquid
lined like Marilyn, Sofia Loren. She's
beautiful, always looks high.
Peonies and poppies, koi and flowering
vines on her soft shoulders, American thighs.
She has freckles, a little lisp. Angela,
from Wisconsin, who was in the Army
eight years. *This is what a veteran looks like
now*, I keep telling myself, on the sidewalk
after her shift while she drinks, talks
about driving trucks into Baghdad, rolls
her eyes about the VA, being brave. She laughs
about self-medicating PTSD, how the earthquake
the other day made her think *IED*.
I light her cigarette, laugh with her,
squeeze her elbow, thinking *Fucking A*.

After Hours in the Alembic

I turn off the outside lights and Josey
brings in the chalkboard. Last Call
at the Alembic, a Monday, no one here
but us. Josey shakes me an agricole daiquiri
with La Favorite, a Chartreuse float, and then
she burns the ice. When the Kold-Draft works
she makes the best Old Fashioned in the country;
with it busted, she makes the tenth best.
Double counting stacks of twenty-five ones,
a wet bar cloth for our fingers, our lips shifting
for the count. She tips out the bar back
fifteen percent, then gives Carla half, puts half
in her wallet, puts the drop in the hopper in the top
of the safe. Once it's done we sit
at one of the nine tables, play Yahtzee, share
the beers she needs to learn, say *juniper*, say
oak, scotch barrelled, extra hop.

Married

You, you, you, my most
beloved beloved. Keeper of secret
shames: my jealousies, catty
me, writ small. You deserve
better than tears, puny
humanness. Train windows
full of green
and golden fields,
slow-cooker full of soup, vintage
crystal chilled for you,
come home.

But with each
scrubbed floor, each elaborate
retelling of each erotic dream—*It was you,
but it wasn't you*—come three tedious
recountings of what student said what
when. Ten emails, forwarded
without comment, our shared rolled eyes
implied.

For better or worse. For root
canal, for laughing on the high
speed ferry to the cape. My mouth
on your neck, say. My hand on your
emerald-cut calf.

Ten linear feet
of scraped, sanded, and caulked porch
rail, freshly primed balustrade. Clean
plates. A half gallon of organic
two percent. Love poems, a dime
a dozen. Everything,
better and worse.

Lightning Source UK Ltd.
Milton Keynes UK
UKOW04f0328290415

250552UK00002B/42/P